Studies in 2 Timothy

By Michael Penny

I0159615

ISBN: 978-1-78364-520-6

www.obt.org.uk

****

The Open Bible Trust
Fordland Mount, Upper Basildon,
Reading, RG8 8LU, UK.

Studies in 2 Timothy

Contents

Page

Introduction

Introduction

The *best* introduction to these studies would be an earlier book of mine entitled *Timothy: The Man*. However, one cannot assume that the reader has a copy of this available so what follows is a précis of the things said in that book.

Paul

The author of 2 Timothy was the Apostle Paul. He wrote 13 letters, or 14 if he wrote Hebrews. Seven of these were written during the period of time covered by the Acts of the Apostles; seven were written afterwards. Most conservative scholars suggest four of these last seven were written during his two year house arrest mentioned in Acts 28:30 and three a little later.

Written *during* the Acts Period	Written *after* the Acts period
Galatians	Ephesians
Hebrews	Colossians
1 & 2 Thessalonians	Philemon
1 & 2 Corinthians	Philippians
Romans	1 Timothy
	Titus
	2 Timothy

From this, then, it would appear that 2 Timothy was Paul's *last* letter. In fact, if we accept the martyrdom of John, spoken of by our Lord in Matthew 20:22-23 and Mark 10:35-40, as having taken place in about AD 62, then 2 Timothy is, in fact, the last New Testament document to have been written. (For more on John's martyrdom see Appendix 2 of *Approaching the Bible* by Michael Penny.)

Paul and Timothy

Timothy lived in a town called Lystra in Galatia and Paul met him there on his second missionary journey (Acts 16:1-5). By this time Timothy was already a believer and the Christians there spoke well of him. He had a Jewish mother who had omitted having him circumcised when a child, because she was married to a Greek. This would mean that Timothy would not be an acceptable witness to the Jews who had not yet come to believe that Jesus was the Christ, the Son of God. Thus Timothy, a young man possibly in his later teens, was willing to undergo circumcision in order to accompany Paul. This, in itself, speaks of his genuine commitment. From that point onwards, Paul and Timothy were almost inseparable, unless Paul sent him to do some task or other, or Paul was in prison, although Timothy sought him out whenever he could.

Timothy accompanied Paul on his second missionary journey. They travelled throughout the region of Phrygia and Galatia and on to Troas, where they may well have met Luke. From there they crossed into Europe, visiting first Philippi, where Paul and Silas were imprisoned. Then came Thessalonica where some of the Jews who did not accept what Paul taught about Jesus of Nazareth being the Christ (Messiah) and the Son of God, rushed upon the house where they thought he was staying. At night the Christians there sent him off to Berea where many of the Jews believed and all seemed to be going well, until Jews from Thessalonica came over and started to stir things up. Paul was immediately sent by boat to Athens. Timothy, along with Silas, was left in Berea to carry on the work.

When Paul was in Athens, Timothy journeyed to him with news of what was happening further north. Paul, however, was concerned about the Thessalonian Christians and so sent Timothy to them, to strengthen and encourage them (1 Thessalonians 3:1-5). Paul moved on to Corinth and while there Timothy returned with good news (3:6).

When Paul was in Corinth, initially he had to work, making tents, to support himself. However, once joined by Timothy and Silas, he was able to devote himself exclusively to preaching, presumably because Timothy and Silas could undertake work of some nature to support the three of them. After some time, Paul left Corinth, leaving Timothy and Silas there to carry on the work of preaching and teaching (Acts 18:1-5,18; 2 Corinthians 1:18-19).

And if we continue reading through the Acts of the Apostles, and through the earlier letters of Paul, this same picture is repeated. And then, at the end of Acts, Paul arrives in Rome as a prisoner, and spends two years under house arrest, waiting for his hearing. Early on he wrote Ephesians, but Timothy is not mentioned. Shortly afterwards he wrote Colossians and Philemon, and we see that Timothy is there, with him. Towards the end of those two years he wrote Philippians. Timothy is still with him, but Paul is about to send him to Philippi. This is Paul's testimony about Timothy.

> I hope in the Lord Jesus to send Timothy to you soon, that I also may be cheered when I receive news about you. I have no one else like him, who takes a genuine interest in your welfare. For everyone looks out for his own interests, not those of Jesus Christ. But you know that Timothy has proved himself, because as a son with his father he has served with me in the work of the gospel. I hope,

therefore, to send him as soon as I see how things go with me. (Philippians 2:19-23)

"I have no one else like him." He "takes a *genuine* interest in your affairs". "Timothy has *proved himself.*" "*As a son with his father* he has served with me in the work of the gospel." What testimonies!

It seems that Paul was released from that first imprisonment and when free saw Timothy at Ephesus (1 Timothy 1:3). However, a little while after that meeting he felt it necessary to write to Timothy as he was concerned about him. From reading 1 Timothy it seems that Timothy had lost some of his enthusiasm and in one place Paul told him "Do not neglect your gift, which was given to you through a prophetic message when the body of elders laid their hands on you" (1 Timothy 4:14). What gift this was, we cannot be sure, but during the Acts period each believer had some gift or other (1 Corinthians 12:7-11). However, most of these ceased at the end of Acts (1 Corinthians 13:8), but some continued for a while; Ephesians 4:11 lists apostles, prophets, evangelists, pastors and teachers which were given "until" (Ephesians 4:13) the Jewish and Gentile Christians of that time reached "unity in the faith and in the knowledge of the Son of God". Thus Timothy's gift may well have been one of those, possibly that of pastor and teacher. However, it seems he was not using that gift.

Not long after writing 1 Timothy and Titus, Paul was rearrested and wrote 2 Timothy. As we shall see, Paul's first letter did not seem to have had the desired effect and here he told Timothy to "fan into flame the gift of God, which is in you through the laying on of my hands" (2 Timothy 1:6).

Applications

All of us who have been in the Christian faith for some while will have had the sad experience of seeing those who were once keen, losing their enthusiasm. How do we deal with them? What do we say? In this letter of Paul we may well find many things which will help us.

2 Timothy
Chapter 1

2 Timothy
Chapter 1

1:1: **Paul, an apostle of Christ Jesus by the will of God, according to the promise of life that is in Christ Jesus.**

Paul introduces himself as "an apostle of Jesus Christ". He was chosen and 'sent' by Christ. Initially there were twelve (Acts 1:26), but others were added, including Paul and Barnabas (Acts 14:1-4,14; see also Romans 16:7). And the ascended Christ commissioned many others and it seems that each church had an apostle (1 Corinthians 12:28; Ephesians 3:5; 4:11). However, Paul is the only one termed the "apostle to the Gentiles" (Romans 1:5; 11:13; Galatians 2:8). He was chosen, commissioned and sent by Christ, in accordance with the will of God and according to the life, the eternal life, that is in Christ Jesus. And this eternal life, this salvation, is found in no one else, for there is no other name under heaven given to men by which we must be saved (Acts 4:12).

1:2: **To Timothy, my dear son: Grace, mercy and peace from God the Father and Christ Jesus our Lord.**

Although Paul refers to Timothy as a 'son' in a number of other places, this is the only place where he called him "my *dear* son". This shows Paul's affection for Timothy, even though Timothy appears less enthusiastic for Christ and for Paul than he once was.

'Grace' and 'peace' commence all Paul's letters, with the exception of Hebrews. 'Grace' is the Greek *charis* and means 'undeserved merit'. One acronym for 'grace' is:

God's
Riches
At
Christ's
Expense.

Before God could give us what we do not deserve – forgiveness, eternal life, righteousness, all spiritual blessings, etc., etc, etc. – as a holy and righteous God the penalty for all our sins had first to be paid. That penalty was paid by Christ when He became the Lamb of God who took away the sin of the world. Once the sin issue had been dealt with, God could then be gracious. '*Charis*', or 'Grace', was the usual Greek greeting, although it certainly did not have the fullness of meaning that Christians gave it.

'Peace' is the Greek *eirene*, equivalent to the Hebrew *shalom*. It means much more than the absence of war, or the absence of hostility, or the absence of anything bad. When a Jew greeted another with '*Shalom*', he was expressing the desire that the person may experience all God's goodness. Thus in combining 'grace and peace' Paul was bringing together the usual Greek and Hebrew greetings, making a new, fuller Christian one.

However, in both of his letters to Timothy Paul introduces a third word, 'mercy'. Vine defines this as "an outward manifestation of pity; it assumes need on the part of he who receives it, and resources adequate to meet that need on the part of him who shows it." Paul may well have been able to show mercy and grace to Timothy, as well as bringing him peace. However, the grace, mercy and peace that Paul extends to Timothy is "from God the Father and Christ Jesus our Lord". Only they could meet and satisfy the needs that Timothy had at that point of time.

***1:3-4:* I thank God, whom I serve, as my forefathers did, with a clear conscience, as night and day I constantly remember you in my prayers. Recalling your tears, I long to see you, so that I may be filled with joy.**

Here Paul thanks God for Timothy as he 'constantly' remembers him in his prayers. Paul also, at times, 'constantly' prayed for the Romans and Thessalonians, and did not stop praying for the Ephesians and Colossians (Romans 1:9; 1 Thessalonians 1:3; 2:13; 2 Thessalonians 1:11; Ephesians 1:16; Colossians 1:9). I say 'at times' because some, having read these words, feel they have to 'constantly' pray all of the time for all sorts of people. However, when people who are dear to us are having serious problems we naturally pray for them continually. The injunction to "pray continually" (1 Thessalonians 5:17) is correct, but most of us seldom have a need to continually pray for the same people or persons.

Paul 'longs' to see Timothy, not only because of the condition Timothy now finds himself in but because the last time they had met there had been tears. This possibly was when Paul left Timothy in Ephesus and he went on to Macedonia (1 Timothy 1:3-4). Then Paul left Timothy the task of dealing with so-called Christians who taught false doctrines, myths and genealogies, and who, as a result, promoted controversy. Maybe Timothy felt he wasn't up to the task and wanted Paul to remain. His stomach problems and frequent illnesses could not have helped (1 Timothy 5:23).

1:5-6: **I have been reminded of your sincere faith, which first lived in your grandmother Lois and in your mother Eunice and, I am persuaded, now lives in you also. For this reason I remind you to fan into flame the gift of God, which is in you through the laying on of my hands.**

Paul now strikes another positive note describing Timothy's faith, in spite of whatever problems he had, as being 'sincere', and comparing it to the faith of both his grandmother and mother. Also, again in spite of whatever problems Timothy was going through, Paul was 'persuaded' that that faith was still alive in Timothy. Because Paul was persuaded that that sincere faith was still there, he 'reminded' Timothy to fan into flame his God-given gift.

Paul had mentioned this in his first letter, telling Timothy not to "neglect your gift, which was given you through a prophetic message when the body of elders laid their hands on you" (1 Timothy 4:14). Clearly Paul was one of those elders and in 2 Timothy 1:6 Paul personalizes this by just mentioning himself as laying hands on Timothy. Timothy seems not to have responded to Paul's earlier letter and plea. Would this more personal one work?

But what was Timothy's gift? It seems that during the period of time covered by the Acts of the Apostles each believer was given a special gift by the Holy Spirit, received through the laying on of hands by an apostle (e.g. Acts 8:17; 19:6; Romans 1:11). These gifts were many and varied.

> Now to each one the manifestation of the Spirit is given for the common good. To one there is given through the Spirit the message of wisdom, to another the message of

knowledge by means of the same Spirit, to another faith by the same Spirit, to another gifts of healing by that one Spirit, to another miraculous powers, to another prophecy, to another distinguishing between spirits, to another speaking in different kinds of tongues, and to still another the interpretation of tongues. All these are the work of one and the same Spirit, and he gives them to each one, just as he determines. (1 Corinthians 12:7-11; see also 12:28-31 and Romans 12:6-8.)

It would seem that the apostles had many gifts (2 Corinthians 12:12), but the majority of Christians had but one and it was not intended that such miraculous gifts would continue forever. Faith, hope and love were to remain, but not the gifts. Love was the greatest and love was not to fail, "but where there are prophecies, they will cease; where there are tongues, they will be stilled; where there is knowledge, it will pass away" (1 Corinthians 13:8,13).

The purpose of these miraculous signs is best expressed by John, at the end of his gospel. He wrote:

Jesus did many other miraculous signs in the presence of his disciples, which are not recorded in this book. But these are written that you may believe that Jesus is the Christ (Messiah), the Son of God, and that by believing you may have life in his name. (John 20:30-31)

One reason for the miraculous signs was so that the people of Israel would know that Jesus Christ fulfilled the Messianic prophecies (e.g. Isaiah 35:4-6). Thus when, at the end of Acts, Israel, as a nation, had hardened their hearts so much against this message, they became blind and deaf, God's salvation was sent directly to the Gentiles (Acts 28:25-28). It would seem that this was the point when most of the miraculous gifts ceased, but not all. In the last letters of Paul there is very little of the miraculous. However, a few gifts continued for a while, but for a very different reason.

> It was he who gave some to be apostles, some to be prophets, some to be evangelists, and some to be pastors and teachers, to prepare God's people for works of service, *so that* the body of Christ may be built up until we all reach unity in the faith and in the knowledge of the Son of God and become mature, attaining to the whole measure of the fullness of Christ. (Ephesians 4:11-13)

Thus these apostles, prophets, evangelists, pastors and teachers were to continue until those Jewish and Gentile Christians of that time reached a unity in the faith and became mature. This was linked to knowing Jesus Christ as the Son of God.

As for Timothy, it is possible that his gift was that of a teacher, although it may have been that of a pastor or even an evangelist. However, whichever it was, he was not using it, and one possible suggestion as to why he was struggling with his faith was that he had not been healed of his stomach problems and frequent illnesses (1 Timothy 5:23). Not only would such a condition be debilitating, Timothy may have felt aggrieved because he was not healed. (For more on the miracles of the Acts period, their purpose and significance see *The Miracles of the Apostles* by Michael Penny.)

1:7: **For God did not give us a spirit of timidity, but a spirit of power, of love and of self-discipline.**

The work of the Holy Spirit does not cease, even though it may change. People still need His power if Christ is to dwell in their hearts through faith, and if they are to grasp how wide and long and high and deep is the love of Christ, and if they are to know and acknowledge that love in their lives (Ephesians 3:16-19). With the indwelling Spirit there is no reason for timidity. The power of God which raised Christ from the dead is available to believers, (Ephesians 1:19-20), enabling us to love others and to have the self-discipline to overcome the trials and tribulations, the difficulties and disappointments, of this life.

1:8-9a: So do not be ashamed to testify about our Lord, or ashamed of me his prisoner. But join with me in suffering for the gospel, by the power of God, who has saved us and called us to a holy life - not because of anything we have done but because of his own purpose and grace.

"So ….." wrote Paul, because God did not give us a spirit of timidity, but one of power, love and self-control, "….. do not be ashamed to testify". It strikes me that in John 7:45-52 Nicodemus may have been somewhat timid in his defence of the Lord. Maybe he was even a little ashamed, but at least he did speak up and say something. No doubt many of us have, at times, been equally timid in not speaking up when we should have. Maybe we were worried about what others would think. This may be understandable for a new believer, but Timothy, by this time, had been a believer for about fifteen years. However, if the reason we kept silent was because we were ashamed of the Lord, then we seriously need to think about our Christian commitment.

Paul exhorted Timothy not to be ashamed of testifying about Christ, and also told him not to be ashamed of Paul the prisoner. Are we sometimes ashamed to be identified with Christian leaders? For me, that depends. There are many worthy ones with whom we should be glad to be identified, even though I may not fully agree with them. However, there are others today whose doctrines and ethics are not in harmony with the Scriptures and with whom I have to strongly disagree and with whom I do not want to be identified.

In earlier years Timothy had been eager to be identified with Paul in earlier imprisonments. However, things were now tougher. Nero Caesar was on the throne and Christians were being persecuted, imprisoned, put to death. Maybe Timothy wanted to distance himself from Paul. Maybe he was concerned about his own well-being, even his life. Paul exhorts him to face whatever suffering there may be in store for him. Face it for the sake of the gospel. If you proclaim the gospel, you may suffer, but the gospel will spread, people will be saved. If you don't proclaim the gospel, you may not suffer, but what will happen to the gospel? And what is 'the gospel'? Paul speaks of this gospel in the opening verses of 1 Corinthians 15 and then spells it out very clearly and simply.

> For what I received I passed on to you as of first importance: that Christ died for our sins according to the Scriptures, that he was buried, that he was raised on the third day according to the Scriptures. (1 Corinthians 15:3-4)

This 'gospel' is of "first importance" and Paul was not ashamed of the gospel, because it is the power of God for the salvation of everyone who believes: first for the Jew, then for the Gentile (Romans 1:16). And it is the "power of God" which will enable Timothy to cope with any sufferings. God has saved us and "called us to a holy life", and part of the 'holy life' may be suffering, and if it is, His power will enable us to cope with that suffering. Timothy had known this in the past. He had been in prison himself (Hebrews 13:23) some years earlier, but now he was older, probably in his earlier thirties, and his health was not what it had been. None-the- less, it was still pertinent to live a holy life.

Holiness is a difficult idea for some people. There are two aspects to it. First of all, when we believe the gospel of salvation we are sealed with the Spirit of God (Ephesians 1:13-14). God then separates us to Himself and we become holy in His sight (Ephesians 1:4; Colossians 1:22). However, there is still the injunction for us to be holy (1 Peter 1:15-16), and we do so by putting to death whatever belongs to our earthly nature, and by getting rid of all such things as "anger, rage, malice, slander and filthy language" (Colossians 3:5,8). It seems then that there are two aspects to holiness: in God's eyes believers are already holy because Christ has taken away their sins. However, their response to this is to live in the way that God would have them live, by giving up certain ways and adopting others. All Christians need to avoid the acts of the sinful nature and exhibit the fruit of the Spirit (Galatians 5:19-25). This is what Paul wanted Timothy to do.

God has saved people and called them to a holy life, not because of any good thing they may have done. As Paul puts it in Ephesians 2:8-10:

> For it is by grace you have been saved, through faith - and this not from yourselves, it is the gift of God - not by works, so that no one can boast. For we are God's workmanship, created in Christ Jesus to do good works, which God prepared in advance for us to do.

And although there may be other things that God has prepared for people to do, I am convinced that the good works that He desires from Christians is to follow the ethical and moral instructions in the Bible which lead to a holy life. It is by grace that we are saved through faith, and His purpose for us is that we lead a holy life.

1:9b-10: **This grace was given us in Christ Jesus before the beginning of time, but it has now been revealed through the appearing of our Saviour, Christ Jesus, who has destroyed death and has brought life and immortality to light through the gospel.**

Jesus Christ is described as the Lamb slain from the creation of the world (Revelation 13:8) and here we see that grace was part of God's plan even before the beginning of time. These two – grace and Christ's sacrifice for sin – go hand in hand: for a holy and righteous God the former is impossible without the latter. To be just, God has to justify sinners and He has done just that, (Romans 3:26). However, even though there was grace in the Old Testament under the law, true grace did not come until Jesus Christ (John 1:17). Jesus Christ, by His sacrifice for sin and by His resurrection destroyed death, showed that life was possible after death, thus bringing immortality to light. This immortal life is available to all "through the gospel". We are saved by grace "through" faith in Christ Jesus.

1:11-12: **And of this gospel I was appointed a herald and an apostle and a teacher. That is why I am suffering as I am. Yet I am not ashamed, because I know whom I have believed, and am convinced that he is able to guard what I have entrusted to him for that day.**

Paul was chosen by God to be His "chosen instrument to carry my name before the Gentiles and their kings and before the people of Israel" (Acts 9:15). As such he was an apostle, and he is the only apostle called 'the Apostle to the Gentiles'. He was a herald; taking the gospel to places it had never been taken to before. And he was a teacher, whenever possible staying in places for long times to teach the people and returning to them to see how they were doing.

However, it was because of the gospel that he was suffering; suffering at the hands of the Jews, the Romans and the Greeks. The Jews opposed him, both non-Christian and Christian Jews. The non-Christian Jews disagreed that Jesus was the Christ, the Son of God. They hounded Paul out of city after city, abusing him, even stoning him. A section of Jewish Christendom did not fully understand the gospel. These were the Judaisers, Christian Jews who insisted that the Gentiles had to be circumcised to be saved and also had to keep the Law of Moses. They undid much of Paul's initial work and caused him extra work and great heartache. He wrote in his letters about it, e.g. see Galatians. He went to Jerusalem to discuss it, see Acts 15. He revisited places he had been to before, no doubt correcting such wrong teaching.

The Romans had initially left Paul and Christians alone. They saw Christianity as part of Judaism, which it was. Acts period Christianity was initially the fulfilment of the promises of the Old Testament. It was not until God revealed the secret mystery of Ephesians at the end of Acts and did something new that Christianity developed into something quite different. Then the Romans in general, and Nero Caesar in particular, became hostile and, at the time of writing 2 Timothy, Paul was under arrest, in prison, and sentenced to death.

The opposition from the Greeks was somewhat different. It was more scorn and ridicule, epitomized by the concluding remarks of his meeting with the Areopagus in Athens, when he met and debated with the philosophers. All was going well until he mentioned God raising Christ from the dead. "When they heard about the resurrection of the dead, some of them sneered" and although others said "We want to hear you again on this subject", no further opportunity was afforded (Acts 17:32).

However, in spite of all the opposition and suffering, Paul was **not** ashamed! Why not? And here he writes words which have comforted people throughout the centuries, including hymn writer Daniel Webster Whittle, who wrote the words of the hymn *I know not why God's wondrous grace to me has been made known*, the chorus of which reads:

> But, 'I know whom I have believed;
> And am persuaded that He is able
> To keep that which I've committed
> Unto Him against that day.'

The old hymn writer, following the *KJV*, uses the word 'persuaded'. The *NIV* is closer to the original meaning, using 'convinced'. Paul was convinced. He wanted Timothy to be convinced. And we need to be convinced. Faith is not some wishy-washy idea or feeling. "Faith is being *sure* of what we hope for and *certain* of what we do not see" (Hebrews 11:1). This is the faith that Abraham had and to which Paul refers in Romans 4:18-22.

> Against all hope, Abraham in hope believed and so became the father of many nations, just as it had been said to him, "So shall your offspring be." Without weakening

in his faith, he faced the fact that his body was as good as dead - since he was about a hundred years old - and that Sarah's womb was also dead. Yet he did not waver through unbelief regarding the promise of God, but was strengthened in his faith and gave glory to God, being *fully persuaded* that God had power to do what he had promised. This is why "it was credited to him as righteousness."

Abraham was "fully persuaded that God had the power to do what he had promised". That is true faith. Paul had it and was convinced, fully persuaded, that God would guard all that Paul had entrusted to Him. Timothy needed to be fully persuaded of this also, and so do we. We need have no doubts at all that God loves us, that Christ died for us, that we are forgiven and that we will be raised from the dead to enjoy an eternity with our heavenly Father. He will guard all that we have committed to Him.

1:13: What you heard from me, keep as the pattern of sound teaching, with faith and love in Christ Jesus.

Paul then told Timothy to keep as a pattern of sound teaching that which he had heard Paul teach. That, too, is good advice to us. As we have mentioned before, Paul is the only person called 'The Apostle to the Gentiles' thus it is more important for us to know, understand and follow his teaching than it is to follow that of Peter, James and John. It is true that we need all the Bible if we are to understand God's plans and purpose for mankind, and we can learn from all Scripture because "All Scripture is God-breathed and is useful for teaching, rebuking, correcting and training in righteousness, so that the man of God may be thoroughly equipped for every good work" (2 Timothy 3:16-17).

However, all Christians give more weight to the New Testament than the Old. None of us sees the need to offer animal sacrifices. The Bible is a progressive revelation from God and as Gentiles it is right and proper for us to give greater weight to what God says to and about Gentiles. It is also sensible to give greater weight to the later parts of the New Testament, and to give greater weight to Paul's later letters than to his earlier ones.

When stating the above, some people get quite concerned, as we seem to be putting Paul and his letters above Christ and the gospels. This is not the case. Jesus Christ is the centre of Paul's ministry. He exalts Christ as much as, if not more than, any other New Testament writer. Three Christ-exalting passages from his later letters are Ephesians 1:19-23, Philippians 2:6-11 and Colossians 1:15-20. We need to recognise that Christ is the Lamb of God who takes away the sin of the world. There is salvation in no one else.

However, the Bible tells us that "Jesus Christ has become a *servant of **the Jews*** on behalf of God's truth, to confirm the promises made to the patriarchs" (Romans 15:8), or as the *KJV* puts it, "a minister of the circumcision". This will explain why our Lord had little to do with Gentiles while on earth. It also explains His battles with the Pharisees over the Mosaic Law. He came and taught a people who were under that Law, and that may be why we find some of what He taught difficult to understand and impossible to do. The fact is the Gospels are the accounts of Christ's time on earth, by three people who knew Him and by one who did not. They contain what Christ did, taught and what He wanted the Jews to do.

The earlier letters of Peter, James, John, Jude and Paul are accounts of the crucified, risen, ascended, glorified Christ and contain what He wanted the Jewish and Gentile Christians of the Acts period to do. The later letters of Paul contain what that same glorified Christ required of Christians in the post-Acts period. This is why we find the teaching and instructions in such letters as, say Titus, much easier to understand and put into practice than those in, say, Hebrews. Thus let us keep as the pattern of sound teaching the latest revelation God gave to mankind, that contained in Paul's later letters.

However, we should keep it with faith and love in Christ Jesus. Faith means being fully convinced, and we should be fully convinced about the special position Paul's writings hold for Gentiles. But we must also keep it with love. Earlier Paul had written to the Ephesians telling them, "live a life worthy of the calling you have received". And they were told how to do this: by being "completely humble and gentle; be patient, bearing with one another in love." They were also told to "Make every effort to keep (guard, *KJV*) the unity of the Spirit through the bond of peace" (Ephesians 4:1-3). Next Paul told Timothy to guard something else.

1:14: Guard the good deposit that was entrusted to you - guard it with the help of the Holy Spirit who lives in us.

Here Timothy is told to guard 'the good deposit', but what is that 'good deposit'? The word 'deposit' occurs rarely and on each of its previous occurrences always refers to the Holy Spirit Himself.

> Now it is God who makes both us and you stand firm in Christ. He anointed us, set his seal of ownership on us, and put his Spirit in our hearts as a *deposit*, guaranteeing what is to come. (2 Corinthians 1:21-22)

Now it is God who has made us for this very purpose and has given us the Spirit as a *deposit*, guaranteeing what is to come. (2 Corinthians 5:5)

And you also were included in Christ when you heard the word of truth, the gospel of your salvation. Having believed, you were marked in him with a seal, the promised Holy Spirit, who is a *deposit* guaranteeing our inheritance until the redemption of those who are God's possession - to the praise of his glory. (Ephesians 1:13-14)

We read that the Thessalonians were told not to quench the Spirit (1 Thessalonians 5:19; *KJV*), and maybe Paul was concerned that Timothy would do likewise; that he would not fan into flame the gift he had been given by God. However, Timothy is told to guard this good deposit "with the help of the Holy Spirit" thus it seems unlikely that the good deposit refers to the Spirit himself. And this should not surprise us as in the above three references the word translated 'deposit' is the Greek *arrabon.* However, in 2 Timothy 1:14 it is *parakotatheke*, a word which occurs again at the end of 1 Timothy. There Paul gives a similar charge; "Timothy guard what has been entrusted to your care" (1 Timothy 6:20). So what has been entrusted to Timothy's care? What is the good deposit?

The subject of this section is 'the gospel' and it seems that 'the gospel of salvation by grace through faith' is the good deposit, rather than any other body of teaching. Of this gospel he says that he was a herald, an apostle and teacher. He was suffering because of the gospel and he wanted Timothy to share in those sufferings. In 1 Corinthians 15:3 he describes the gospel as of "first importance", and later he tells Timothy to "do the work of an evangelist" (2 Timothy 4:5). There can be no doubt about it that the core of Christianity is this gospel and we need to guard it with the help of the Holy Spirit who lives in us. There are many teachings in Christianity over which we can agree to differ; the gospel is not one of them.

1:15: You know that everyone in the province of Asia has deserted me, including Phygelus and Hermogenes.

Here we have a sad statement; all in Asia had deserted Paul. If, as suggested earlier, John had been martyred in about AD 62, this statement will not be such a great surprise. John had written Revelation earlier, to the seven churches in Asia, and already there were serious problems in those churches. After his two year imprisonment Paul had visited Ephesus and maybe some of those churches mentioned by John. It would appear that he did not receive the warmest of welcomes. As to who were Phygelus and Hermogenes, we know nothing. This is the only mention of them in the New Testament.

1:16-18: May the Lord show mercy to the household of Onesiphorus, because he often refreshed me and was not ashamed of my chains. On the contrary, when he was in Rome, he searched hard for me until he found me. May the Lord grant that he will find mercy from the Lord on that day! You know very well in how many ways he helped me in Ephesus.

Similarly with Onesiphorus: 2 Timothy contains the only two references to him. 2 Timothy 4:19 sends greetings to "the household of Onesiphorus". We know nothing of him, other than what we have here. It appears that he, but not his household, may also have deserted Paul – or perhaps he had died. However, earlier he had been proud to be associated with Paul. He had refreshed Paul and he had searched for Paul during that two-year period of house arrest (Acts 28:30). And he had helped Paul in many ways when Paul was in Ephesus. Clearly Paul had not forgotten this Christian service and wrote, "May the Lord grant that he will find mercy from the Lord on that day!"

2 Timothy
Chapter 2

2 Timothy
Chapter 2

2:1-2: **You then, my son, be strong in the grace that is in Christ Jesus. And the things you have heard me say in the presence of many witnesses entrust to reliable men who will also be qualified to teach others.**

Here, again, Paul refers to Timothy as his 'son', and he wants him to "be strong in the grace that is in Christ Jesus". There are other ideas of grace in religious circles, other than that which is in Christ Jesus. One idea of grace is that as long as we do one act of kindness in our lives, then God will grant us forgiveness. In some branches of eastern religions, grace is secured by buying fish or birds from the priest and then letting them go. And we must not forget that in some branches of Christendom a sacrament is said to be a means of grace; i.e. grace is obtained by baptism or the mass or confession or being anointed with oil etc.

Indeed all these *are* ideas of grace, for if God did forgive us our sins and grant us eternal life because we had done one kind thing, or had bought birds and let them go or because we had been baptized or made a confession, etc., then that would, indeed, be gracious of Him. However, none of these things is what the Bible teaches about grace. The grace of God is found in Christ Jesus alone, because the only way a holy and righteous God can freely forgive sinners is if the penalty for those sins has been paid, and that is just what Jesus did as the Lamb of God who took away the sin of the world. Thus salvation by grace through faith in the Lord

Jesus Christ is *the* grace that Timothy had to be strong in, and so do we.

We need to understand why "the grace that is in Christ Jesus" is the only grace possible for a holy and righteous God. And we need to pass it on to others, especially to those who are reliable and able to teach others also. They also need to know and be able to teach the other truths that Paul taught. As Paul is the only person called 'The Apostle to the Gentiles' it seems eminently sensible that we who are Gentiles should have a good understanding of the ministry and teaching given to him by the risen and glorified Saviour.

2:3-7: **Endure hardship with us like a good soldier of Christ Jesus. No one serving as a soldier gets involved in civilian affairs - he wants to please his commanding officer. Similarly, if anyone competes as an athlete, he does not receive the victor's crown unless he competes according to the rules. The hardworking farmer should be the first to receive a share of the crops. Reflect on what I am saying, for the Lord will give you insight into all this.**

By way of encouragement, or exhortation, Paul gives Timothy three examples. First there is the soldier: he is told to endure hardship as a 'good' soldier of Christ Jesus. Was Timothy finding the hardships of his day too much for him, especially with his stomach problems and frequent illnesses? And a 'good' soldier will always want to please his commanding officer. Was Timothy caring more about pleasing other people, those around him, those not Christians? If so, he needed to be more like Peter and John in Acts 4:19-20 who decided they had to obey God rather than the Jewish ruling council. And a 'good' soldier will not get entangled with civilian affairs. Was this part of Timothy's problems? Was he being side-tracked into what we may call 'public service'?

The next example is that of an athlete, who must compete according to the rules. False starts, handing over the baton outside of the box, running round the hurdles or jumps, taking short cuts; all these will lead to a disqualification. An athlete must compete according to the rules of that race. And of course, the rules may change from one race to another; the start of a marathon is very different from the start of a sprint. And rules may vary from country to country, although with international athletics that, now, is unlikely. However, it is essential for success that athletes know the rules for the race they are competing in. Similarly, it is essential for Christians to know the rules for today's race.

To be following the rules of the Mosaic Law in an age of grace would be inappropriate. To follow the rules our Lord Jesus gave the Jews when He was on earth, will cause us difficulties. To follow the rules He gave for those Jewish and Gentile Christians of the Acts period will cause problems. It is important to follow the rules for the age of grace in which we live and these are set out in the revelation the ascended Christ gave to the Apostle Paul and are found in those last seven letters. Of course some of the rules are the same in all dispensations, but which ones? Some change, but which ones? We need to study the rule-book to find out. In that way we are more likely to win the race.

The last example is that of a 'hardworking' farmer. The one who digs the soil deeper, plants the seeds more carefully, waters the plants more thoroughly; he is the one who will be the first to see his plants reach maturity and have a good harvest.

However, Paul is not going to push this any further with Timothy. He simply says, "Reflect on what I am saying, for the Lord will give you insight into all this." A similar situation arose with the Philippians when he was writing to them about the prize which can accompany salvation, a subject which can be quite contentious in Christian circles even today. Having written on the subject, Paul then says, "All of us who are mature should take such a view of things. And if on some point you think differently, that too God will make clear to you" (Philippians 3:15). All too often we can take discussions over doctrines too far. Sometimes it is better to leave them with the Lord.

2:8-10: Remember Jesus Christ, raised from the dead, descended from David. This is my gospel, for which I am suffering even to the point of being chained like a criminal. But God's word is not chained. Therefore I endure everything for the sake of the elect, that they too may obtain the salvation that is in Christ Jesus, with eternal glory.

Paul, yet again, returns to the gospel and the resurrection of Christ. This was what was most on his mind. He tells Timothy to 'remember' it and, as suggested earlier, it is this 'gospel' which is the 'good deposit' that Paul wants Timothy to guard. It was because of this gospel that Paul was suffering, even to being chained like a criminal in prison. The Jews would not accept Jesus as the Son of David, the Christ (Messiah) and the Son of God. The pagans would not accept that He rose from the dead. Paul was being hounded on both sides yet even though he was chained, God's word was not chained. Paul was writing letters, and those letters were being read and circulated (e.g. Colossians 4:16). Other people had written about Christ and, as I have suggested, this second letter to Timothy may well be the last New Testament document to be written. These gospels and letters contained the Word of God and the gospel message was not chained.

During his first imprisonment, some two or three years earlier, Paul had written about those who preached Christ out of envy, rivalry and selfish ambition, even hoping to add to Paul's troubles while he was in prison. Paul's attitude to this was, "What does it matter? The important thing is that in every way, whether from false motives or true, Christ is preached. And because of this I rejoice" (Philippians 1:15-18).

Thus we can see that Paul did more than "endure everything", he rejoiced. He rejoiced when the gospel was preached, for how else would people be saved? He rejoiced when people were saved. Whether he was free or in prison, he rejoiced. Whether he was preaching the gospel or someone else was, he rejoiced. If the courage he showed while suffering in prison encouraged others to witness, he rejoiced. He just wanted others to obtain salvation and to share in the eternal glory which was already his.

2:11-13: **Here is a trustworthy saying:**
> **If we died with him, we will also live with him;**
> **if we endure, we will also reign with him.**
> **If we disown him, he will also disown us;**
> **if we are faithless, he will remain faithful,**
> > **for he cannot disown himself.**

Paul writes a number of 'trustworthy sayings'; see 1 Timothy 1:15; 3:1; 4:9; 2 Timothy 2:11; Titus 3:8. This one is probably the longest and may represent an early statement of faith. The opening phrase is "If we died with him, we will also live with him". This is practically the same wording as Romans 6:8 and is the same teaching as in Romans 6:5 where we read, "If we have been united with him like this in his death, we will certainly also be united with him in his resurrection." This is an example of the doctrine of 'identification'. When we believe that Christ died for our sins, we become identified with Him in His death. As such, the penalty for our sins has been paid and we are forgiven and saved. We are also identified with him in resurrection and so are guaranteed eternal life. Just as He rose from the dead, so will we. Thus if we died with Him, we will also live with Him.

The next statement is, "If we endure, we will also reign with him". Paul uses the word 'endure' four times in this letter, though not always the same Greek word. First he exhorts Timothy to endure hardship as a good soldier (2:3) He then states that he endures everything for the sake of the elect (2:10) and reminds Timothy of what he had to endure in Antioch, Iconium and Lystra (3:11). And the last reference, like the first, encourages Timothy to endure hardship (4:5). But why endure all these things? Because if we do, we will also reign with Christ. There is eternal life for all who believe Christ died for their sins and rose again on the third day. However, there is something added – a reward, a crown, a prize – for those who endure. (For more on this subject see *Gifts and Rewards from God* by Michael Penny.)

However, if we disown Him, He will disown us (see also Matthew 10:33). Timothy was in danger of not enduring the hardships of Christianity. He was in danger of disowning Christ. If he did so, Christ would disown Him, but what does that mean? Having believed the gospel of salvation we are sealed with the Holy Spirit of God who is a deposit guaranteeing our inheritance (Ephesians 1:13-14). The gospel is by grace so that it can be guaranteed (Romans 4:16; 2 Corinthians 1:22; 5:5; Ephesians 1:14). Works cannot guarantee anything; only grace can. As such, if we have been identified with Christ in His death, we shall certainly be united with Him in His resurrection. Thus what does 'disown us' mean? The next phrase may throw some light on the subject.

"If we are faithless, he will remain faithful, for he cannot disown himself." Thus if a person ceases to be faithful to the Lord and becomes faithless, none-the-less, Christ remains faithful. On believing in Christ we become His children and He cannot deny Himself. Our salvation is guaranteed. Our eternal life is safe and secure, but what about the reigning? What about the crown, the prize, the reward? Can that be denied? Paul put it clearly in 1 Corinthians 3:11-15.

> For no one can lay any foundation other than the one already laid, which is Jesus Christ. If any man builds on this foundation using gold, silver, costly stones, wood, hay or straw, his work will be shown for what it is, because the Day will bring it to light. It will be revealed with fire, and the fire will test the quality of each man's work. If what he has built survives, he will receive his reward. If it is burned up, he will suffer loss; he himself will be saved, but only as one escaping through the flames.

To endure may be likened to building with gold, silver and costly stones, materials which will stand the test of fire. If a believer's service contains such enduring materials, he will receive some reward. However, if he is faithless, if his building is constructed solely of wood, hay and stubble, he will suffer the loss of that reward, but not the loss of eternal life. God is faithful to His promises. He will not disown His children eternal life. However, He will disown them the reward. They will have their eternal life, but they will not share in the reign.

2:14: **Keep reminding them of these things. Warn them before God against quarrelling about words; it is of no value, and only ruins those who listen.**

Paul then exhorted Timothy to remind people of these important lessons. However, he was also to warn them against the over use of semantics, the quarrelling and arguing over words. What is its value? We are not likely to convince anyone to our way of thinking if the debate sinks to the level of debating the root meaning of Greek or Hebrew words. And what about those who are listening? The likelihood is that they will get confused, and it could ruin their faith.

The gospel of Christianity is simple to explain and understand; the holy life is again explained in straightforward terms. There may be a place for mature believers to debate amongst themselves Calvinism v Armenianism, or the pros and cons of Premillennialism, Postmillennialism and Amillennialism, but not in front of others who are not equipped for it.

2:15: **Do your best to present yourself to God as one approved, a workman who does not need to be ashamed and who correctly handles the word of truth.**

We come now to a verse which is very well known in some Christian circles but which, in my opinion, is very much misunderstood. The understanding of this verse generally comes from the *KJV*.

KJV	American Standard Version	NIV
Study to shew thyself approved unto God, a workman that needeth not to be ashamed, rightly dividing the word of truth	Give diligence to present thyself approved unto God, a workman that needeth not to be ashamed, handling aright the word of truth.	Do your best to present yourself to God as one approved, a workman who does not need to be ashamed and who correctly handles the word of truth.

The interpretation of those who base their understanding upon the *KJV* is that this verse teaches that approval from God is based upon studying the Bible, and rightly dividing the Bible, but is that correct? The expression 'word of truth' occurs elsewhere in the New Testament and we shall look at all its occurrences to see if we can ascertain to what Paul is referring when he uses the expression. Is it the Bible? There are just three other references:

Ephesians 1:13-14: And you also were included in Christ when you heard *the word of truth*, **the gospel of your salvation**. Having believed, you were marked in him with a seal, the promised Holy Spirit, who is a deposit guaranteeing our inheritance until the redemption of those who are God's possession - to the praise of his glory.

Colossians 1:5-6: the faith and love that spring from the hope that is stored up for you in heaven and that you have already heard about in *the word of truth*, **the gospel** that has come to you. All over the world **this gospel** is bearing fruit and growing, just as it has been doing among you since the day you heard it and understood God's grace in all its truth.

James 1:18: He chose to give us birth through *the word of truth*, that we might be a kind of firstfruits of all he created.

From the first two quotations it is very clear that 'the word of truth' is 'the gospel of salvation', and from James we see that 'the word of truth' is linked with the new 'birth'. The Bible itself does not give us that new birth, as the Lord told the Pharisees.

> You diligently study the Scriptures because you think that by them you possess eternal life. These are the Scriptures that testify about me, yet you refuse to come to me to have life. (John 5:39-40)

Diligent study of the Scriptures did not gain these people God's approval. As Paul wrote in 2 Timothy 3:15, the Scriptures are able to make us wise to salvation, but that salvation comes through the gospel, through faith in the Lord Jesus Christ. Thus it seems to me that in 2 Timothy 2:15 we are told that God's approval comes from the diligent way in which we handle the gospel of salvation. If we handle that correctly, we have nothing to be ashamed of. The Bible is important and we need to study it, but our Lord is more concerned about the way in which we present the gospel of grace, than He is about which method of systematic theology we use.

2:16-18: **Avoid godless chatter, because those who indulge in it will become more and more ungodly. Their teaching will spread like gangrene. Among them are Hymenaeus and Philetus, who have wandered away from the truth. They say that the resurrection has already taken place, and they destroy the faith of some**.

What is 'godless chatter'? Is it talking about football, music, a holiday, and such like? As long as such things are kept in perspective and discussed decently, I cannot see how these can come into the category of 'godless chatter' that will make us more ungodly.

Certainly obscenity, sexual innuendos, coarse joking and the like are, and Ephesians 5:4 makes it clear that these are out of place and such things will lead us away from the holy life. But the example given here is of two people, of whom we know nothing else, who said that the resurrection was a past event. These may have been Greeks, influenced by the philosophy of their day.

We remember that the Greek philosophers in Athens sneered at Paul when he told them of Christ's resurrection (Acts 17:30-32). Belief in a physical resurrection was a problem to the Greek thought of that day. Some regarded physical matter as evil, thus to think of the holy Son of God as being physically raised from the dead was a barrier to them. And as for thinking that Christians, at some time in the future when Christ returns, would be raised from the dead clothed with Christ righteousness and equipped with a resurrection body like His .... Well, that was just untenable to those who saw matter as evil. To such people the future resurrection of believers was replaced with the view that it represented the spiritual new birth experienced in the past when a person believed the gospel. As such they missed the truth for themselves and also upset the faith of others.

We may not look upon this as 'godless' chatter, but this is the example Paul gives and may partially explain why he wrote to the Corinthians as he did on the issue of resurrection (1 Corinthians 15), that city being so close the Athens, the centre of Philosophy.

However, the main reason why this is termed 'godless' chatter may have been because their views were based upon a world view which did not have God in the equation, or at least one that could not take into account that God can give life to the dead (Romans 4:17) and "is able to do immeasurably more than all we ask or imagine" (Ephesians 3:20). And it may be that certain schemes of 'theology', which do not accept the literal and physical resurrection of Christ, may come into the category of 'godless chatter'.

2:19: **Nevertheless, God's solid foundation stands firm, sealed with this inscription: "The Lord knows those who are his," and, "Everyone who confesses the name of the Lord must turn away from wickedness."**

Paul next returns to his two major themes. God's foundation is Jesus Christ (1 Corinthians 3:11). He is the solid rock and, as the Lamb of God who took away the sin of the world, He laid the foundation for grace. Those who accept Him as their Saviour, and believe the gospel of salvation, are sealed with the Spirit and so the Lord knows those who are His. These are called upon to turn away from wickedness and to live a holy life. The two – the gospel and the holy life – are the basis of Christianity.

2:20-22: In a large house there are articles not only of gold and silver, but also of wood and clay; some are for noble purposes and some for ignoble. If a man cleanses himself from the latter, he will be an instrument for noble purposes, made holy, useful to the Master and prepared to do any good work. Flee the evil desires of youth, and pursue righteousness, faith, love and peace, along with those who call on the Lord out of a pure heart.

Paul now uses a different illustration; that of gold and silver utensils, as opposed to those made of wood and clay. He is trying all the ways he knows to motivate Timothy.

In a big house the gold and silver articles would be on display and would be for the use of the master, his family and guests. The wooden and clay ones would be for the kitchen and garbage, and for use by the servants. Paul wanted Timothy to be like a golden or silver utensil, one that the Lord, the Master of the house, would want to use, and that should be our desire too. We want to be used by the Master. But what are we made of? Gold and silver, or wood and clay?

To be fit for the Master's use we need to build with gold, silver and precious stones, not with wood, hay and stubble (1

Corinthians 3:10-15). We need to be prepared to do any good work, however menial, even washing feet. We need to flee the desires of youth, whether they are immoral or simply inappropriate for the good soldier and winning athlete (2 Timothy 2:4-5). We need to obey our commanding officer, compete according to the rules, be like a hardworking farmer, and all these we can achieve by pursuing righteousness, faith, love and peace. That will give all servants of the Lord a pure heart. In this I am reminded of Ephesians 4:1-3, where Paul exhorts his readers to live a life worthy of the calling they have received. This they could achieve by being "completely humble and gentle, being "patient, bearing with one another in love" and by making "every effort to keep the unity of the Spirit through the bond of peace".

2:23-26: **Don't have anything to do with foolish and stupid arguments, because you know they produce quarrels. And the Lord's servant must not quarrel; instead, he must be kind to everyone, able to teach, not resentful. Those who oppose him he must gently instruct, in the hope that God will grant them repentance leading them to a knowledge of the truth, and that they will come to their senses and escape from the trap of the devil, who has taken them captive to do his will.**

Having told Timothy to pursue righteousness, faith, love and peace, Paul told him next to have nothing to do with foolish and stupid arguments. What, precisely, Paul had in mind is impossible to say. However, in his first letter to Timothy he links these with false doctrines and quarrels about words (1 Timothy 6:3-5; see 2 Timothy 2:14), and Titus is told to "avoid foolish controversies and genealogies and arguments and quarrels about the law" (Titus 3:9).

Rather than arguing and quarrelling, the Christian must be kind to everyone. Kindness is more likely to win a person to the Christian point of view than arguing. He must be able to teach and if any disagree or argue against him, there is no room for resentment. In fact any opposition must be dealt with gently. Having explained the gospel, we should leave it there and not push it further or become involved in an argument. We should leave the person to the Lord in the hope that he will repent and come to a knowledge of the truth. If he does he will escape the devil's clutches.

> As for you, you were dead in your transgressions and sins, in which you used to live when you followed the ways of this world and of the ruler of the kingdom of the air, the spirit who is now at work in those who are disobedient. All of us also lived among them at one time, gratifying the cravings of our sinful nature and following its desires and thoughts. Like the rest, we were by nature objects of wrath. But because of his great love for us, God, who is rich in mercy, made us alive with Christ even when we were dead in transgressions - it is by grace you have been saved. (Ephesians 2:1-5)

Kindness and gentleness are greater catalysts for repentance than arguments and quarrels.

2 Timothy
Chapter 3

2 Timothy
Chapter 3

3:1: **But mark this: There will be terrible times in the last days.**

When some people see the words 'last days' they automatically think that they refer to the years leading up to the return of our Lord Jesus. However, in the publication *The Last days! When?* each and every occurrence of the expression is studied and we discover that this is not the case. That is why some translations, and even the *NIV* in some places, use the expression 'days to come' instead of 'last days'. Thus Paul was letting Timothy know what he could expect in 'days to come', in the days after Paul was gone, in the days when he would be on his own. Some of it may be applicable to the days leading up to the second coming, but that is a secondary issue. So, what lay ahead for Timothy?

3:2-5: **People will be lovers of themselves, lovers of money, boastful, proud, abusive, disobedient to their parents, ungrateful, unholy, without love, unforgiving, slanderous, without self-control, brutal, not lovers of the good, treacherous, rash, conceited, lovers of pleasure rather than lovers of God - having a form of godliness but denying its power. Have nothing to do with them.**

The first thing we need to ask about this passage is what people did Paul have in mind? The usual understanding of this passage is that he was talking about the world, people in general, but is that view correct? Those who do not know God are naturally unholy.

Those who do not know God are naturally lovers of pleasure more than lovers of God. Those whom Paul has in mind have a "form of godliness, but deny its power". The world in general does not pretend to have a form of godliness and knows nothing of the power which produced godliness so they cannot deny it.

What may be the situation here is that Paul had in mind the church. That this is what the people in the churches would become. They would not be lovers of God or of the good, but rather they would be lovers of themselves, lovers of money, and lovers of pleasure. Can church people get like that?

They would be unholy, ungrateful and unforgiving. They would be proud, boastful and conceited. They would be abusive and rash, slanderous and treacherous. They have no self-control and will not even listen to their parents. They will have a form of godliness, but will deny its power by the way they live their lives. The true power of God is available to all believers (Ephesians 1:19-20) and that power works in their hearts to change and alter them, enabling them to love others (Ephesians 3:16-19).

Thus one can only conclude that these are the wolves in sheep's clothing that the Lord warned about in Matthew 7:15, and of whom Paul warned the Ephesian elders (Acts 20:29-30); people who, for one reason or another, come into the church. Their motives may be to gain a following, as Paul states in Acts 20:30. In the past homosexuals entered the Catholic priesthood so that they could hide their sexuality. Today paedophiles target small churches and young people's organisations, often volunteering to work with the children. This may be an extreme example, but it shows that we cannot assume that everyone in our churches is a true believer.

Some Christians would list liberal theologians as those who have a form of godliness but who deny the power, for some deny the virgin birth, the miracles and the physical resurrection. Although I would strongly disagree with them over their teaching on such issues, I cannot attribute to the vast majority of them such words as lovers of money, boastful, proud, abusive, ungrateful, unforgiving, slanderous, brutal, treacherous, rash, conceited, and the like.

However, about these people Paul gave Timothy one simple instruction: "Have nothing to do with them". What can you do with people like that? And there is more to come about their influence over other people.

3:6-7: They are the kind who worm their way into homes and gain control over weak-willed women, who are loaded down with sins and are swayed by all kinds of evil desires, always learning but never able to acknowledge the truth.

'Weak women' in the Greek is *gunaikaria*, "a diminutive expressing contempt" (*New Bible Commentary*), showing just what Paul felt about such people. The *Amplified Version* expands these verses as follows:

> For among them are those who worm their way into homes and captivate silly *and* weak-natured *and* spiritually dwarfed women, loaded down with [the burden of their] sins, [and easily] swayed *and* led away by various evil desires *and* seductive impulses. [These weak women will listen to anybody who will teach them]; they are forever inquiring *and* getting information, but are never able to arrive at a recognition *and* knowledge of the Truth.

The conclusion drawn is that these people, although always learning, are "never able to *acknowledge* the truth", "never able to arrive at a recognition and *knowledge* of the truth".

The word for knowledge / acknowledge here is *epignosis*. *Gnosis* is 'knowledge'; *epignosis* is 'deeper knowledge' or 'acknowledgement'; i.e. putting it into practice. One of the features of the post-modernist culture in which we now live is that we can expect a greater interest in religion, of all sorts, but we cannot expect a great commitment. In other words people read all sorts of religious books and they may even attend church, but their commitment to Christ and their involvement within the church may well be lacking.

3:8-9: Just as Jannes and Jambres opposed Moses, so also these men oppose the truth - men of depraved minds, who, as far as the faith is concerned, are rejected. But they will not get very far because, as in the case of those men, their folly will be clear to everyone.

One of the Jewish *Targums*, commenting on Exodus 7:11, tells us that Jannes and Jambres were the two magicians in the service of the Pharaoh who opposed Moses (Exodus 7-9). These people were powerful and could emulate some of the initial miracles Moses performed. Even though the Lord Himself does mention those who perform false miracles (see Matthew 7:22-23), and Paul wrote about the "counterfeit miracles, signs and wonders" in the days just prior to the second coming (2 Thessalonians 2:9), there is no hint in the list given in 2 Timothy 3 of these people having miraculous ability.

The issue here is opposition. They opposed Moses; these people will oppose the truth. They are men of depraved minds and as far as the faith is concerned, they are rejected. They are rejected quite simply either because they have no faith or because they have a distorted or false faith (James 2:14).

Paul then stated that such men would not get very far, quite simply because their deeds will not match their words. "By their fruit will you recognise them", said the Lord (Matthew 7:16), and their fruit is described as "folly" and will be recognisable by all believers. These are the type of people who await Timothy in "days to come".

3:10-11: **You, however, know all about my teaching, my way of life, my purpose, faith, patience, love, endurance, persecutions, sufferings - what kinds of things happened to me in Antioch, Iconium and Lystra, the persecutions I endured. Yet the Lord rescued me from all of them.**

In contrast to these people stood Paul. Timothy could compare these people with Paul. He had known him and worked with him for fifteen years or so. He knew about his teaching and his way of life and could see that they matched. He knew Paul's purpose was to preach Christ crucified and at first hand Timothy had seen his faith and love in practice. He had seen his patience and endurance, and had witnessed some of the persecutions and sufferings Paul experienced, especially those in Antioch, Iconium and Lystra (e.g. see Acts 13:49-52; 14:5-6,19-20; and see also 2 Corinthians 11:23-28). Paul's faith was genuine. The Lord had rescued and enabled Paul, and the Lord could rescue and enable Timothy.

3:12-13: **In fact, everyone who wants to live a godly life in Christ Jesus will be persecuted, while evil men and impostors will go from bad to worse, deceiving and being deceived.**

However, Paul was not the only one to have suffered. Many others had already done so and many more were to do so. In fact Paul made it quite clear to Timothy that everyone who lived a godly life in Christ Jesus will be persecuted. Even though he wanted Timothy to rekindle the flame and fan into flame the gift he had been given, he was honest with him as to what lay ahead, just as the Lord had been with Paul (Acts 9:15-16).

The last days, these 'days to come' for Timothy, would be difficult. Good living Christians were to suffer; yet evil people would go from bad to worse. And society would deteriorate for the result of this evil was that people would not only deceive others, they would themselves be deceived. Once a sufficient number of people cheat and steal, those who cheat and steal are cheated and stolen from. Once enough people give bad service in their work, they end up receiving bad service themselves.

3:14-15: **But as for you, continue in what you have learned and have become convinced of, because you know those from whom you learned it, and how from infancy you have known the holy Scriptures, which are able to make you wise for salvation through faith in Christ Jesus.**

As for Timothy, Paul wanted him to continue in what he had learned and been convinced of, because Timothy knew those from whom he had learned it. First of all there was his mother and grandmother. Then there was Paul, and also Silas with whom Timothy had done much work. And although his mother had not had him circumcised when a baby, she had taught him the Scriptures, and he had known them from infancy. His mother and grandmother, Paul and Silas, and the Scriptures, were all in harmony in what they taught. And Timothy was a Christian. He knew the salvation there was through faith in Christ.

3:16-17: **All Scripture is God-breathed and is useful for teaching, rebuking, correcting and training in righteousness, so that the man of God may be thoroughly equipped for every good work.**

"All Scripture is God-breathed." "Men spoke from God as they were carried along by the Holy Spirit", wrote Peter (2 Peter 1:20-21). As such, not only are the Scriptures able to make us wise to salvation, they are also useful for teaching, rebuking, correcting and training in righteousness. What is right and wrong? Is something moral or immoral? How do we decide? Do we take what the minister or priest says? Do we follow what some book or magazine advocates? Do we go with the teaching of the church or chapel? Or some bishop or archbishop? No! Not unless they are in accord with what the Scriptures teach.

What is God's will? We will find the vast majority of the answers to such a question in the Bible. It is the Christian's handbook for equipping us to do every good work. What are those "good works, which God prepared in advance for us to do"? (Ephesians 2:10.) We will find the answer to that question in the Scriptures. The good works God wants us to do are clearly stated there, just as the wrong ones are, which He does not want us to do.

2 Timothy
Chapter 4

2 Timothy
Chapter 4

4:1-2: **In the presence of God and of Christ Jesus, who will judge the living and the dead, and in view of his appearing and his kingdom, I give you this charge: Preach the Word; be prepared in season and out of season; correct, rebuke and encourage - with great patience and careful instruction.**

This last chapter opens with a solemn charge. "I give you this charge", wrote Paul, "In the presence of God and Christ Jesus, who will judge the living and the dead." In other words, Paul is reminding Timothy that his Christian service will not be judged by Paul, but by the Lord Himself at His appearing, and Timothy's reward in eternal life will depend upon how faithful that service has been.

The charge Paul lays on Timothy is to "Preach the Word; be prepared in season and out of season; correct, rebuke and encourage - with great patience and careful instruction." In many ways this summarises much of what Paul has previously written. Perhaps it is also a good outline of what we should do.

We may well be prepared to preach the word and encourage people. We may well strive to do so with great patience and careful instruction. But how many of us relish the prospect of correcting and rebuking fellow-Christians at a personal level, especially those who are close to us? Or, come to that, how many of us would accept being corrected and rebuked by others in our local church?

It is not easy in our society and perhaps the most acceptable way of doing it today is to let the Bible do it for us. If we simply teach what the Bible teaches and show people what it says, that may be best for it is the Bible which is useful for "teaching, rebuking, correcting and training". Having done that it may then be best to simply leave the people with the Lord for Him to give them insight (2 Timothy 2:7).

4:3-4: For the time will come when men will not put up with sound doctrine. Instead, to suit their own desires, they will gather around them a great number of teachers to say what their itching ears want to hear. They will turn their ears away from the truth and turn aside to myths.

One reason for Paul's solemn oath to Timothy is the urgency of the situation. "The time will come," wrote Paul, "when men will not put up with sound doctrine." And that is exactly the situation we find towards the end of the first century AD and on into the second. As we have seen, Paul's great concern was for the gospel of salvation by grace through faith in the Lord Jesus Christ. Yet when we read the early church fathers, we see an almost complete absence of this fundamental teaching. There is no clear message of salvation. It seems to be one of works in which martyrdom seems the only assured way of gaining eternal life.

It seems that there was to come a time when people would not listen to sound doctrine based upon the Scriptures, but rather would prefer to listen to someone who would say the things they wanted him to say. In this way people would not be challenged. What was it Paul wrote earlier? "Always learning but never able to acknowledge the truth" (2 Timothy 3:7). These people are different.

They purposely turn their ears away from the truth. They want to hear only what they want to hear and so turn aside from the truth of Scripture to follow myths. Do we have a similar situation today? Do people want sound doctrine? Do people like comforting messages, telling them what they want to hear? Are there myths out there that people like to hear? The wishy-washy views of some New Age teachers makes me wonder what appeal they have, but they do have great appeal because people do not want to hear firm views and clear teaching. They want to believe what they want to believe, and to do what they want to do. The Christian cannot be like that.

4:5: But you, keep your head in all situations, endure hardship, do the work of an evangelist, discharge all the duties of your ministry.

People are much more likely to keep their heads, whatever the situation, if they are gentle and humble rather than if they argue or quarrel. It is often pride which turns a debate into an argument and an argument into a quarrel.

Timothy is exhorted, yet again, to endure hardship. As Christians we are not likely to have to endure any hardship compared to what lay ahead for Timothy. However, we have to endure being a marginalized group in a materialistic post-modern society. How do we cope and deal with the problems such a society throws at us? These we need to endure, with gentleness and humility.

Timothy is told to do the work of an evangelist, a proclaimer of the good news, a preacher of the gospel, a teacher of the fact that Christ died for our sins and rose again on the third day. That gospel was sneered at by the Greeks, so it was no easy task. In our materialist scientific society we, too, will meet opposition.

However, like Timothy, we need to discharge all the duties required of us and surely one common to us all is to share the gospel.

4:6-8: For I am already being poured out like a drink offering, and the time has come for my departure. I have fought the good fight, I have finished the race, I have kept the faith. Now there is in store for me the crown of righteousness, which the Lord, the righteous Judge, will award to me on that day - and not only to me, but also to all who have longed for his appearing.

Paul wanted Timothy to take on all the duties of his ministry because Paul was already being poured out like a drink offering. He knew the time of his death was imminent. Who else could take over his mantle? Would Timothy do it? Did he?

Paul had fought a good fight. He had run the race according to the rules and had finished the course. Throughout he had kept the faith. As a result there was in store for him a crown of righteousness, a crown that he had won: a crown that would be awarded to him by the righteous Judge. I am so glad that the Holy Spirit inspired Paul to write those words for if Paul had not won the prize, the reward, the crown, what hope would there be for any of us? And the fact is that the Lord is going to award many more crowns. All those who long for His appearing shall receive one. To long for His appearing, to yearn for His second coming, shows a great depth of faith, love and commitment. If Christ returned tomorrow all my understanding of prophecy would be wrong, and I would be delighted! As John says, "Come, Lord Jesus!" (Revelation 22:20).

4:9-13: **Do your best to come to me quickly, for Demas, because he loved this world, has deserted me and has gone to Thessalonica. Crescens has gone to Galatia, and Titus to Dalmatia. Only Luke is with me. Get Mark and bring him with you, because he is helpful to me in my ministry. I sent Tychicus to Ephesus. When you come, bring the cloak that I left with Carpus at Troas, and my scrolls, especially the parchments.**

Paul wanted Timothy to come to him as soon as possible. One cannot help but feel for Paul. He had been arrested and imprisoned. He had had his first hearing and it had not gone well. He was concerned about Timothy. He was concerned about all the Christians, especially those in Asia who had deserted him. Even Demas had gone. He had been with Paul in Rome during his first imprisonment and was with him when he had written to the Colossians (4:14) and to Philemon (v 24). However his love of this world was greater than his love for the Lord and he had gone.

However, I do not have the impression that Crescens and Titus had deserted Paul. It seems that Paul is simply relating to Timothy where people had gone. Crescens, and this is the only mention of him, had gone to Galatia, and Titus to Dalmatia, having, one supposes, completed the work Paul had given him to do on Crete. Luke was still there with him and Paul was eager not only to see Timothy, but also John Mark.

John Mark had been with Paul when they returned to Antioch from Jerusalem. He had started with him and Barnabas on their first missionary journey but, for some reason, left them and returned home (Acts 12:25, 13:5,13). As a result, Paul did not want to take him on his second journey and for that reason he and Barnabas disagreed so strongly that they separated (Acts 15:37-

40). However, all that was many years ago, and in the intervening years Mark had accompanied Peter to Babylon (1 Peter 5:13). Now Paul wanted to see him and he knew Mark would be useful for the work.

Tychicus had been with Paul on his third journey (Acts 20:4) and in Rome with Paul during his first imprisonment. He was with him when he wrote the letters to the Ephesians and Colossians and may well have been the deliverer of those letters (Ephesians 6:21; Colossians 4:7). After his release from prison, he wanted to send him to Titus (Titus 3:12), whether he did or not, we do now know. However, he did send him to Ephesus, which may have been his hometown for we are told that he was from Asia (Acts 20:4).

It seems that winter was approaching (2 Timothy 4:21) and Paul wanted Timothy to bring him his cloak. He also wanted the scrolls and parchments. The Scriptures were written on scrolls and Paul may have wanted a copy of the Scriptures, or it may have been some other writings. Parchment was used for writing letters. Whether Paul wanted blank parchment so that he could write further letters, or whether he was referring to letters he had received, we do not know. However, this indicated that Paul was going to make the most use of his time in prison. He was, in fact, intent on making the most of his remaining days here on earth.

4:14-15: Alexander the metalworker did me a great deal of harm. The Lord will repay him for what he has done. You too should be on your guard against him, because he strongly opposed our message.

We know nothing of this Alexander the metalworker. He may be the same Alexander mentioned by Paul in 1 Timothy 1:20. That

Alexander had rejected Christianity, the prophecies of Paul and had shipwrecked the faith of some. As a result, Paul handed Alexander over to Satan to be taught not to blaspheme, whatever that may mean. Alexander the metalworker did Paul much harm, but we do not know the details, and Paul simply says, "The Lord will repay him for what he has done." Timothy may well have known something about this man and Paul warns him to be on his guard against him, because he strongly opposes the Christian message.

Alexander may possibly have been a metalworker making idols, like Demetrius the silversmith who lived in Ephesus and who made shrines of the goddess Artemis for a living. He led the revolt against Paul in that city (Acts 19:23-41). If so, we can well imagine Alexander's hostility towards the Christian message.

4:16-18: **At my first defence, no one came to my support, but everyone deserted me. May it not be held against them. But the Lord stood at my side and gave me strength, so that through me the message might be fully proclaimed and all the Gentiles might hear it. And I was delivered from the lion's mouth. The Lord will rescue me from every evil attack and will bring me safely to his heavenly kingdom. To him be glory for ever and ever. Amen.**

I do not quite know what Paul means that "no one came to my support", and that everyone had deserted him. Luke was there with him, and it seems he had sent others on various missions. However, what credibility would Luke have in the court of Caesar? Or Titus? Maybe Paul was hoping that some of the Roman citizens who had become Christians, and who were in the church in Rome, would speak up for him. If that were the case, none did! Paul understood the current hostile political situation with Caesar Nero in command. Thus he did not want anything to be held against those who had not had the courage to stand firm.

However, the Lord had stood with Paul and through His indwelling Spirit had strengthened Paul and enabled him to give a good account. As a result a clear gospel message had been declared and all the Gentiles had heard, but more than that, he had been delivered from the lion's mouth, a likely reference to Nero.

But what did Paul mean when he wrote, "The Lord will rescue me from every evil attack"? He cannot mean imprisonments, beatings, stoning, and the many other persecutions that Paul had suffered. It cannot even refer to death, as Paul was expecting to die soon. Or perhaps it does, for Paul had gone through many such trials and tribulations and had come out the other side, probably a better and more sympathetic man, with a greater understanding of human frailty. He had learned the truth of what the Lord had told him, "My grace is sufficient for you" (2 Corinthians 12:9). And so Paul knew that even when the attack of death came, it would be followed by a resurrection, and he would be brought safely into God's heavenly kingdom. The Lord had seen him through every danger upon this earth, and would see him through the greatest danger of all, death. No wonder Paul concludes with the words, "To him be glory for ever and ever. Amen."

4:19-21: **Greet Priscilla and Aquila and the household of Onesiphorus. Erastus stayed in Corinth, and I left Trophimus sick in Miletus. Do your best to get here before winter. Eubulus greets you, and so do Pudens, Linus, Claudia and all the brothers.**

Priscilla and Aquila were Christian Jews who had been expelled from Rome when all the Jews had been expelled. They joined Paul in Corinth and travelled with him to Ephesus where he left them, and were still there when he wrote a letter to the Corinthians. They returned to Rome later when things had calmed down there. (Acts 18:2.18,19; 1 Corinthians 16:19; Romans 16:3). At the time of writing this second letter to Timothy it seems they are not in Rome where Paul was. It seems that they were with Timothy, who was possibly still in Ephesus where Paul had left him (1 Timothy 1:3).

Paul had already mentioned the household of Onesiphorus earlier in the letter (1:16-18). He informed Timothy that Erastus stayed in Corinth. Timothy and Erastus had worked together in Macedonia (Acts 19:22), and when writing to the Romans from Corinth, Paul states that Erastus was the city's director of public works (Acts 16:23). Was this the same Erastus? It seems it was and so we can well understand why we read here that Erastus stayed in Corinth.

Trophimus was from Ephesus and had accompanied Paul on part of his third missionary journey. Indeed he accompanied Paul all the way to Jerusalem (Acts 20:4; 21:29). However, Paul had left him sick in Miletus! I put an exclamation mark because can one imagine Paul leaving anyone sick anywhere during the period covered by the Acts of the Apostles? We need to consider this situation a little more deeply.

Healing was one of the miraculous signs to Israel that showed that Jesus was the Christ, Messiah (Isaiah 35:4-6; John 20:30-31). It also showed to them that He was the One who could forgive sins (Matthew 9:6). During the time covered by the Acts of the Apostles these signs continued, and Paul healed people by sending them a handkerchief (Acts 19:12). However, once Israel had hardened its heart sufficiently against the message of Jesus, they rendered themselves blind and deaf and God's salvation was to be sent directly to the Gentiles (Acts 28:25-28). In those last seven letters we see a distinct lack of the evidential miraculous signs and wonders.

Not only that, we have at least three records of Paul not healing people. We have Trophimus here, we have Epaphroditus in Philippians 2:25-27, and Timothy himself in 1 Timothy 5:23 where advice, rather than a handkerchief, was sent. This change in dispensation resulted in a change of the rules. There were some advantages – there were no longer miracles of judgement where people could be struck ill or even dead. However, there were some disadvantages – people could no longer count on being healed instantly. This may be a contributing factor in Timothy's seeming demise. Not only did he have stomach problems and was frequently ill, which must be debilitating in itself, he may also have felt aggrieved, even angry, with God that he had not been healed.

However, this is the situation we find ourselves in today. It is no longer certain healing from the laying on of hands; rather it is 'pray' and 'may', and either way, we must acknowledge God and give Him the glory. (For more on the significance of healing and the change, see *The Miracles of the Apostles* by Michael Penny. For more on prayer see *Unanswered Prayer* by Neville Stephens and the questions / answer study by Michael Penny entitled *The Place of Prayer in an Age of Grace*: all are available from the Open Bible Trust: see page 40 for details.)

4:22: **The Lord be with your spirit. Grace be with you.**

"God is love", says 1 John 4:8. And because God so loved the world He sent His one and only Son to be the Lamb of God to take away the sin of the world. This atoning sacrifice paid the penalty for sin and allowed the holy and righteous God to be gracious, forgiving, merciful. God may love us, but where would we be if He were not a God of grace. And so it is, that Paul, who experienced the grace of God on the road to Damascus and considered himself the chief of sinners, begins and ends each of his letters with grace.

More in the "Studies in ..." series

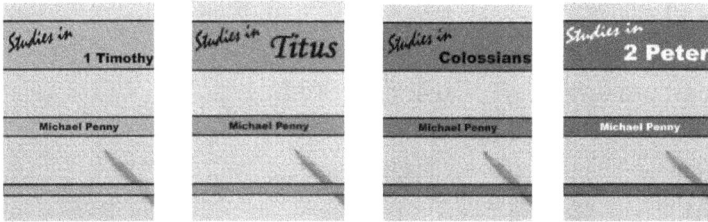

Michael Penny has written, or edited, a number of other books in this series including:

- **Studies in 1 Thessalonians**
- **Studies in 2 Thessalonians**
- **Studies in Colossians**
- **Studies in Philemon**
- **Studies in Philippians**
- **Studies in 1 Timothy**
- **Studies in 2 Timothy**
- **Studies in Titus**
- **Studies in 2 Peter**
- **Studies in John's Epistles**
- **Studies in Jude**
- **Studies in Ruth**

These are also available as eBooks and KDP paperbacks.

Details from www.obt.org.uk

About the author

Michael Penny was born in Ebbw Vale, Gwent, Wales in 1943. He read Mathematics at the University of Reading, before teaching for twelve years and becoming the Director of Mathematics and Business Studies at Queen Mary's College Basingstoke in Hampshire, England. In 1978 he entered Christian publishing, and in 1984 became the administrator of The Open Bible Trust.

He held this position for seven years, before moving to the USA and becoming pastor of Grace Church in New Berlin, Wisconsin. He returned to Britain in 1999, and is at present the Administrator and Editor of The Open Bible Trust. From 2010 he has been Chairman of Churches Together in Reading, where he speaks in a number of churches of different denominations. He is also a member of the Advisory Committee to Reading University Christian Union and a chaplain at Reading College.

He is lead chaplain for Activate Learning and has set up chaplaincy teams in a number of their colleges including Reading College, The City of Oxford College, Bracknell and Wokingham College, and Blackbird Leys College.

He lives near Reading with his wife and has appeared on Premier Radio and BBC Radio Berkshire many times. He has made several speaking tours of America, Canada, Australia, New Zealand and the Netherlands, as well as others to South Africa and the Philippines. Some of his writings have been translated into German and Russian.

Also by Michael Penny

He has written many books including:

40 Problem Passages,
Galatians: Interpretation and Application,
Joel's Prophecy: Past and Future,
Approaching the Bible,
The Miracles of the Apostles,
The Manual on the Gospel of John
The Bible! Myth or Message?

Plus two written with W M Henry:

The Will of God: Past and Present
Following Philippians
Abraham and his seed (with chapters by Sylvia Penny also)

His latest three books are:

James: His life and letter
Peter: His life and letters.
Paul: A Missionary of Genius

Further details of all these books can be seen on

www.obt.org.uk

from where they can also be ordered.

They are also available as eBooks from Amazon and Apple and
as KDP paperbacks from Amazon.

Further Reading

Salvation

Safe and Secure

Sylvia Penny

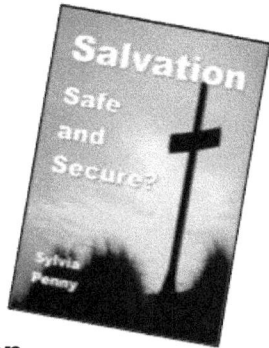

This important book is a thorough treatment of the subject of salvation, asking such questions as ...

- What is it, exactly, that saves us?
- Is salvation secure?
- Can it be lost?
- What is 'conditional security'?

It deals with a wide number of issues such as ...

- Salvation and works
- The doctrine of rewards
- Lordship salvation
- Free grace theology
- Assurance of salvation
- Why people lose their faith

Search magazine

Michael Penny is editor of *Search* magazine.

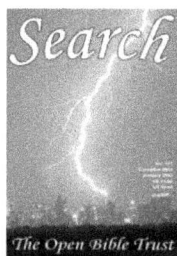

About this book

Studies in 2 Timothy

Paul's second letter to Timothy was the last one he wrote. Paul was back in prison and about to be executed. What was on his mind? What was important? What did he want to tell Timothy, the young man who had been with him for many years and who had proved so useful?

There are words of advice and encouragement for Timothy, in particular, but much of it is so applicable to today. Our society is not so different from the educated, yet barbaric, athletic, yet permissive, Greco-Roman world of the first century. The problems, difficulties and temptations which beset Timothy and others, plague many people today, especially new and young Christians.

The teaching in this letter, together with the other two pastoral Epistles – 1 Timothy and Titus – contain wisdom and advice which are so relevant, and so needed, for Christian leaders and for Christendom today, yet all too often this lovely letter is ignored in Christian circles. This is a shame, because this letter is not a weighty theological epistle, but a letter from an older, mature Christian to a younger one; one whom he dearly loved and cared for.

Publications of The Open Bible Trust must be in accordance with its evangelical, fundamental and dispensational basis. However, beyond this minimum, writers are free to express whatever beliefs they may have as their own understanding, provided that the aim in so doing is to further the object of The Open Bible Trust. A copy of the doctrinal basis is available from

www.obt.org.uk

and from:

THE OPEN BIBLE TRUST
Fordland Mount, Upper Basildon,
Reading, RG8 8LU, UK.